LAKE MICHIGAN

PITT POETRY SERIES   **ED OCHESTER, EDITOR**

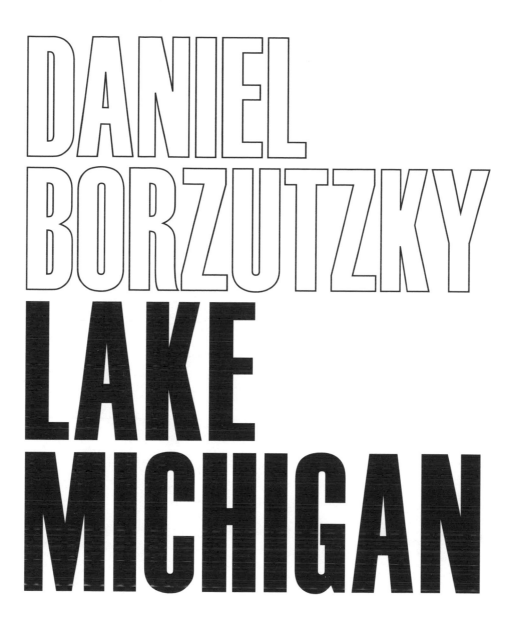

DANIEL BORZUTZKY
LAKE MICHIGAN

UNIVERSITY OF PITTSBURGH PRESS

Published by the University of Pittsburgh Press, Pittsburgh, Pa., 15260
Copyright © 2018, Daniel Borzutzky
All rights reserved
Manufactured in the United States of America
Printed on acid-free paper
10 9 8 7 6 5 4 3 2 1

ISBN 13: 978-0-8229-6522-0
ISBN 10: 0-8229-6522-4

Cover art: Susannah Bielak & Fred Schmalz
Cover design by Joel W. Coggins

To crawl in the mud. To brace oneself in the grease of the mud. To bear.
Soil of mud. Horizon of mud. Sky of mud. Corpses of mud, oh names to warm up in the palm of a feverish breath!

—Aimé Césaire

CONTENTS

LAKE MICHIGAN

Lake Michigan, Scene 0

There are 7 of us in front of the mayor's house asking questions about the boy they shot 22 times

There are 7 of us in front of the mayor's house screaming about how the videotape of the shooting was covered up so the mayor could get reelected

And a police officer says down there where they live there was a shooting   you should be protesting that shooting   a 9-year-old boy was shot by a gangbanger   why aren't you protesting that shooting   why arc you only protesting this shooting

Another police officer wants to know why we are protesting this shooting when just yesterday there was a drive-by shooting in Rogers Park and two innocent bystanders were shot and one of them died

We don't answer   instead we do a die-in in front of the mayor's house and the camera crews from the nightly news stand above us as we lay stiff and motionless on the cold wet pavement

They shot the boy 22 times

They kept the video secret for a year and a fcw days after the video was released we took to the streets and didn't let anyone into the Disney Store

We blocked the doors to Brooks Brothers

We blocked the doors to Topman

The Disney Store was empty but for a few sales folk standing around some Stormtroopers

A guy who drove up from Indiana tried to get into the Disney Store and when we told him that nobody would be buying Stormtroopers today he spat on us and called us stupid assholes

This place is for kids   Y'all are fucked up

We didn't let anyone into the Apple Store

No one got into Banana Republic

A police officer pulled one of us out from in front of Banana Republic and asked us why we weren't protesting the other bodies that were shot by bodies that were not police officers

It was a strange line of questioning

But it kept happening

The cops kept asking why the body they shot was more important to us than the bodies shot by others

Because you took an oath to protect people   we said   not to kill them

Because you are paid to protect people   not to shoot them

Then they filmed us and we were on the nightly news dying-in on the cold wet pavement

And the politicians called us anticapitalist terrorists who wanted to close down the city's access to commerce

Then the public forgot about the boy they shot 22 times and the mayor closed 50 public schools and replaced them with privately run charters

And the mayor said we must make our school system more robust   we must make our schools more efficient   we can no longer have empty schools   we can no longer have failing schools   we can no longer have public schools   we can no longer have public bodies

And he proposed a plan for privatizing all of the bodies of all the residents of Chicago

And the City Council passed the proposal and we were given physical examinations injected with vaccines and told we had quite a bit to learn from those who devoted their lives to prayer   meditation   and nonviolent disobedience

We had no choice

This was the dream they subjected us to

They took us to Lake Michigan   to the prisons on the beach on the northern end of the city   on the border with Evanston   on the sand they imported from Indiana

The police build bonfires to remind us of the bodies they throw into them

They tell us cautionary tales about the secret prison on the West Side where once they killed a man by chaining him to a radiator that fell on his head

They tell us this and they expect us to hate them but when you are a decrepit privatized body who has not been fed for several days it's not always possible to feel something as violent as hatred

And they say   why do you think you are here

And we say   we exist in a historical continuum   our comrades in the 16th century were also not told why they were imprisoned or tarred or killed

And they say   we have video recordings of you torching your neighbors' garages

And they say   we have video recordings of you hiding guns and money under the floorboards of your houses

And they say   where in your heart is love

And we say   it is everywhere   it is all that we have   there is nothing else to hang
on to when you are in the back of a pickup truck handcuffed to other decrepit privatized
bodies rolling around and your heads keep smashing other heads and your shoes keep
kicking other faces and other shoes keep kicking your face and you are bleeding and you
are terrified and you are blindfolded and you are in the back of a pickup truck and no
one has given you enough time to call your father your friend your mother your brother
your lover your x your y you are nothing but a rotten piece of meat   they tell us   as
our broken bodies roll around the back of the truck

This is an attempt to provide context for the insignificant reality of our lives

This is an attempt to provide context for the dreams we have in which we swallow the
bodies of the police officers   the prison guards   the mayor   the migra

These are our dreams   we digest the bodies that destroys us

They throw us in the back of a wagon   take us to a holding cell   and when we are
released we gather in front of the mayor's house

And the police officers say we have better things to do than stand here and make sure
you don't burn down the mayor's house or shoot a journalist or go crazy and shoot
yourselves

Then one of us puts a shoe on the mayor's lawn and they throw her to the ground
put a knee to the back of her neck   handcuff her   tell her she is under arrest for
trespassing

And we all step onto the mayor's lawn and the police officers throw us to the ground
hold their sticks to our necks   put their knees to our backs   pull our hair   handcuff
us   take us to a holding cell where we are separated one from the other and we cannot
call our lawyers   our friends   our families   and we scream from our cells until they
tape our mouths shut

But who will document our deaths and disappearances   we wonder

Who will inscribe our bodies into history

Who will know that at one point in this life we were something other than what the bureaucrats knew us to be

And we are alone for several hours until they bring us trays of stale food and dirty water

A few days pass   we lose track of time   we have no watches   no phones   no way of knowing where we are or what time it is   then an authoritative voice says   take these putrid bodies out to get some sunshine

And we go out into the grass and there is a lawyer and a psychologist and a bureaucrat waiting to interview us   to ask us what it is that we want

We are silent

So they beat us

And when we say please don't beat us they say   finally you are getting the hang of it finally you are learning how to articulate your deepest dreams and desires

And they like this

So they beat us

And when they finish beating us they feed us

And when they finish feeding us they throw dollar bills on the floor and force us to play a game where we must beat each other in order to get the dollar bills and if we don't beat each other they beat us

Sing   they say   or we will beat you

And so we sing what they tell us to sing

We love you   we sing

We love your money   we sing

We love your food   we sing

We love your guns   boots and nightsticks

And they like this song   so they beat us

They pay us and they love us and they beat us

ACT 1

On a Sunday afternoon I reached a lake surrounded by green lawns; in the sunlight
the waters reminded me of silk and floating diamonds; sailing boats were moving over
them. It was the luxury of the Cote d'Azur. . . . There was nothing to remind one of the
squalor with its human wreckage. Crowds of people were sitting on the grass in the
bright sunshine; there were well-behaved loving couples . . . young people had got up a
game of baseball on the lawns; and children were darting in and out of bushes playing
at Indians. . . . A spring day made for leisure. Seagulls flew over the lake and Chicago
appeared as a city huge, wealthy and gay.

—Simone de Beauvoir

le pegaban todos sin que él les haga nada

—César Vallejo

Lake Michigan, Scene 1

They beat me even though I did nothing

I don't know what day it was

But they beat me on the beach

They beat me with iron paws

The mayor ordered the police superintendent to beat me

The police superintendent ordered an officer to beat me

The officer ordered his dogs to attack me

Then someone beat me with iron paws

Then someone kicked me with iron boots

Then someone shot me

Then someone buried me in the sand

Then someone scooped me out of the sand and dumped me somewhere

And I was dead

But I could feel the sand on my body

I could feel the sand filling my mouth

I could feel the sand in my eyes

There was an earthquake in my eyes

There was a tornado in my mouth

But after the storms passed it was peaceful and I was dead

And they beat me even though I did nothing

They said I was illegal

They said I was an immigrant

They said I was an illegal immigrant who roamed the streets in a gang

They said I raped people

They said I killed people

They said I smuggled drugs in my gastrointestinal tract

They said I didn't speak the right language

They said my boss exploited me and I tried to kill him

They said my boss treated me well and I tried to kill him

They said my heart was dark

They said I peddled in blood

They said this is only war and that I had the audacity to think my body could resist the state

Let death come quickly   I asked

Let death be easy

But I did not know how long it would take

I did not know I would be under the sand forever

I did not know that in Chicago the bodies do not die when they have been strangled or riddled with bullets

A journalist asked the mayor why they killed us

I am not responsible   said the mayor

There will be an inquest   said the mayor

We will bring the perpetrators to justice   said the mayor

He was wearing a slim fitting suit and he looked handsome as the hurricane entered his mouth

He was wearing a slim fitting suit and he looked handsome as he pretended he did not live in a city of state-killed cadavers

He had gel in his hair and his shoes were nicely polished

I died and I died again and a voice said something about hope

Another voice said you pay a big price for hope

I dragged myself around the sand and I tried to make it to the water because I thought the water might carry me away but each time I took a step closer to the water the water moved farther from my body and there were faces in the water and they were calling to me and I was trying to get to them

It's what you do when you are dead

But every time I took a step toward the water the water drew farther away

And the faces in the water were murmuring and their murmurs grew louder and louder as I moved nearer and farther

And it is only war   a voice said   by way of explanation   as he photographed my dead body on the sand

And I was dead though I was still breathing when I finally made it to the water

And in the water there was another war going on in the waves

It was only the beginning of the war that would kill me again and again

Lake Michigan, Scene 2

They put paint on my eyes

They put mud on my eyes

They put sludge on my eyes

They asked me to look in a mirror

They said this is your face

They said you have been dead for three days

They said you have been missing for three days

They asked me what I did with my mind

They asked me what I did with my papers

They asked me when I last saw my parents

They asked me what I did with my bank card

They asked me what I did with my hands

I told them my hands were broken

I told them I didn't remember my bank card

I told them about an investigator who came to my office

He worked for the city and his title was Investigator #41

He asked me what I did on the internet

He measured my arms

He measured my legs

He asked me who I spoke to on my cell phone

He asked me who I sent messages to

He asked me if my documents had been filed according to regulation and policy

He looked in my mouth with a flash light

He tested my reflexes

He asked me to stand still   perfectly still   and to keep my balance

I could not keep my balance and he told me he expected me to do better

He asked me why I couldn't keep my balance

He hit me when I tried to keep my balance

He spat on me when I fell to the floor

He kicked me when I fell to the floor

He asked me to stand up   to try to keep my balance

He punched me in the stomach and I fell to the floor and the other workers in the office heard me scream but they could not help me and they were also beaten

He told me I helped an illegal human being and that this made me illegal

He told me I helped an illegal human being find food and as a result I would not be able to eat

He told me I helped an illegal human being drink water and as a result I would not be able to drink water

We got into a van and he took me to the prison on the shores of Lake Michigan and we went into an office and he asked me to sign some papers

I signed nothing and they beat me and locked me in a closet

He took my shirt and pants and locked the door

I sat on the cold ground

I fell asleep

Maybe I died

I woke up and there was a pipe lying next to me

I woke up and there was blood coming out of my mouth

I woke up and I was dead and there was a mountain in the middle of the beach and they took me there

I woke up and I was dead and they left me at the foot of the mountain

I saw a picture of the city in a mirror

I saw giant birds committing suicide

I saw a species of children struck with a terrible plague

They couldn't walk or talk

They crawled and moaned

I asked for money and they gave me a map

I asked for water and they gave me some coins

I asked for my family and they showed me a picture of the mayor

I asked for an attorney and they beat me

I crawled up the mountain and it started to burn

I walked into the flames and I woke up and someone played notes from a ram's horn

I walked out of the flames and fell asleep and I heard my mother's voice

They poured gasoline on me and I recited some numbers in my head

I tasted salt

I tasted gasoline

I heard the children of Chicago crying and they were buried under the mountain

I heard the mayor say our city was a place of sanctuary

I heard the mayor say our city was a shelter for refugees

I saw the police shoot a boy 22 times and I heard the mayor make a promise

Your body will return   he said

Your body will be a dream that spreads slowly across the beach

Your body will be a playground and the children will crawl all over you

I felt my hands burn

I felt my neck burn

I felt my fingers burn

I felt my lips burn

I felt my lungs burn

I felt my elbows burn

I felt my nose burn

My hair was burning and I asked if I could see my sister

They asked me what she looked like and I described her perfectly and they said nothing

I heard them drill into the mountain and it felt like they were drilling into my body

They drilled a hole in the mountain and the children crawled into it and sang a song to the city about how much they loved it

And the song grew softer and softer as the children sang it forever

And it is only war   said a body in uniform

It is only the beginning of war

Lake Michigan, Scene 3

The bodies are on the beach

And the bodies keep breaking

And the fight is over

But the bodies aren't dead

And the mayor keeps saying   I will bring back the bodies

I will bring back the bodies that were broken

The broken bodies speak slowly

They walk slowly onto a beach that hangs over a fire

Into a fire that hangs over a city

Into a city of immigrants   of refugees   of dozens of illegal languages

Into a city where every body is a border between one empire and another

I don't know the name of the police officer who beats me

I don't know the name of the superintendent who orders the police officer to beat me

I don't know the name of the diplomat who exchanged my body for oil

I don't know the name of the governor who exchanged my body for chemicals

The international observers tell me I'm mythological

They tell me my history has been wiped out by history

They look for the barracks but all they see is the lake and its grandeur   the flowering gardens   the flourishing beach

The international observers ask me if I remember the bomb that was dropped on my village

They ask me if I remember the torches   the camps   the ruins

They ask me if I remember the river   the birds   the ghosts

They say   find hope in hopefulness   find life in deathlessness

Locate the proper balance between living and grieving

I walk on the lake and hear voices

I hear voices in the sand and wind

I hear guilt and shame in the waves

I have my body when others are missing

I have my hands when others are severed

I hear the children of Chicago singing   *We live in the blankest of times*

Lake Michigan, Scene 4

A was here

B was here

The dying lake was here

The weeping willow was here

The dead sand was here

The lost coyotes were here

The imported grass was here

The imported beach was here

The tear gas was here

The immigrants exchanged for petroleum were here

The diplomats were here

They looked for us but did not see

They called to us but did not hear

The sweeping wind was here

The purple mouths were here

The nazis were here

The avant-garde was here

The torches were here

The United Nations were here

But our bodies were not badly enough broken for them

The governor was here

The paramedics were here

The first responders were here

The second responders were here

My mother was here

She was looking for my uncle

She was looking for my sister

She was looking for neighborhood kids   friends   acquaintances

A man who came to speak about hope was here

A man who came to speak about forgiveness was here

A man who came to speak about pain was here

The words kept leaving and the refugees from Central America kept coming

The trucks that brought blankets and socks were here

The police and their horses were here

Briefly   the media was here

The investors were here

The economists were here

The street was here

It came onto the beach carrying bodies that howled and hissed

Then peace was here and there were bees and squirrels and rabbits

Then peace was here and a man asked the lord for forgiveness

Then peace was here and a man asked the broken bodies for forgiveness

But we did not forgive him

We refused to forgive him

Forgive us   we said   for not forgiving you

Fuck you   he said   for not forgiving me

And he called us names and beat himself and we were too tired to watch while he wept

We were too tired to think of ourselves and we were too tired to think of another

We were too tired to find ourselves and we were too tired to be found

A cat was here and it devoured a bird

A rat was here and it devoured a rabbit

A man was here and he laughed when we spoke of survival

We looked at the lake and saw a spa full of toxic bacteria

The boats with the prisoners were here and the nazis hissed at them

And we looked at the nazis and we thought about what we could not imagine

And we thought about what we could not imagine and the city refused to feed us unless we forgave it

And we thought about what we could not imagine while the city compared one wound with another   one shrunken bone with another   one broken blankness with another

And a boy-soldier shoved a gag in my mouth and told me he was protecting my mouth from saying the wrong thing   from having to respond when it sees an injustice

From having to scream when it's beaten

From biting through the glands on its tongue

From creating a conflict between language and the impossibility of representation

And the boy-soldier theorized about speech and told me about how he too had sucked on this very same gag   the one that was in my mouth

But then after a few months they took the gag out of his mouth   when his silence had earned him some hope

Lake Michigan, Scene 5

The beach falls

So they say

The infected beach falls sky downward

The city falls under the astral balls

The city sways from one side of the street to the other

The infected beach whines and screeches

The exhaustion of anticipating collapse

The infected beach falls next to another infected beach

The city is bored with forgetting that the chase for victims is not supposed to be boring

The city takes the first shot and the beach crumbles

We don't speak as they shoot or we're beaten

We don't cry as they shoot or we're beaten

The police photograph the dying beach before it sinks

The beach gets closer to the bottom

The beach falls and falls and the city tells us that from now on our names are no longer our names

The city screams to the dying beach   Stop! Being! Dead!

The city empties its glocks into the beach and weeps

The city lights candles   sings ceremonial songs to commemorate its own death

The story begins and ends with the infected beach collapsing

Because the beach is dead the city can now love itself

Because the beach is dead the city can now see itself as a helpless victim of history

The waves are howling

The sand is howling

We cheer for the dying beach because if we don't cheer the city beats us

It starves us

It shoves septic things into our noses and mouths

The city keeps smashing the dying beach

Smashing and smashing till the sand and the rocks are obliterated

It says to the dying beach   don't die we love you so much

But the beach keeps dying

And the city keeps shooting it

And we pray that when the sun comes up we will have another beach

And I pray that when the sun comes up I will have another body

After Plato threw the poets out of The Republic some were sent to countries where they kill you and others were sent to countries where they couldn't give a fuck about the stupid shit poets have to say

The dying beach swirls in the wind

A creek grows out of the sand but it's quickly exterminated

The middle of the story keeps asking to become the end

But form cannot contain the burden of the dying beach

There are no rocks to sit on anymore

There are only dead fish   ash   holes where once there was sand

Lake Michigan, Scene 6

The golden sand of Lake Michigan was here

The chromium spilled from the US Steel plant in Portage, Indiana was here

The raw sewage was here

The animal waste was here

The waters that in the sunlight reminded Simone de Beauvoir of silk and flashing diamonds were here

The seagulls were here

The liquid manure was here

The birds colonized by E. coli were here

The police removing the homeless bodies on the beach were here

The police removing the illegal immigrants on the beach were here

The police beating the mad bodies on the beach were here

The public hospitals were not here and the police had nowhere to take the sick ones to so they kicked them in the face   handcuffed them and took them to jail

A woman screamed and the external police review board heard nothing

No one heard the woman screaming and no one saw the children vomiting

No vomiting children   wrote the external review board   no dead or decaying animals

The members of the external police review board belong to the Democratic Party and they love to play with their children on the beach

They belong to the ACLU and they love to play with their pets on the beach

They volunteer at their kids' schools and they don't believe in the bones of the disappeared

The pigs colonized by E. coli were here

The cattle colonized by E. coli were here

The humans colonized by E. coli were here

The police were here and they murdered two boys and the external police review board saw nothing

Lake Michigan, Scene 7

Here is a body they imported from Guadalajara

Look how good it is at not moving

Here is a body they imported from Guatemala

Look how good it is at not moving

Here is a body they imported from Vietnam

Look how good it is at not moving

Here is a body from the Avondale neighborhood on the Northwest Side of Chicago

Look how good it is at not moving

Here is a body from Humboldt Park

Here is a body from Englewood   La Villita   Back of the Yards   Auburn Gresham
Garfield Park

Pretend you are like pieces of candy   sing the police officers to the bodies they force
to play dead

Pretend you are like pieces of fruit

Pretend you are yellow and orange and red and purple

Pretend you are grape and cherry and lemon and watermelon

Don't move motherfuckers   say the authoritative bodies   as if talking to the cutest of babies or kittens

Don't move or we will bite your candy ass heads off

You are dead and you don't have hands   say the authoritative bodies to the prisoners

You are dead now and this beach is your mass grave

And we will toss you into the bonfire and you will be twigs

And you will nourish the flames

So don't move

Because if you move then we will have to acknowledge that you are rats

You are copulating little rats   say the authoritative bodies in their baby-cute voices

Silence

The police officers and their superiors do not speak

They walk through the maze of dead-playing bodies

They prod the dead-playing bodies with long sticks

They prod the dead-playing bodies with their leather boots

Because if they move the authoritative bodies will be commanded to toss them into the lake

Because if they move the authoritative bodies will be commanded to unzip their pants and piss on the prisoners while singing "God Bless the Child" in the sweetest of voices

Is this enough?

Have you had enough of this game?

These questions are not rhetorical

They are scripted

The police officers wait for a response that does not come

The prisoners also have instructions

Imagine snow melting in the marrows of your bones

Imagine an endless thread of melted wax sewn through your cheek

Imagine your body as a roll of flesh balled up behind the endless bed that is this beach

The prisoners play You're Dead on the beach for several hours while the police officers listen to music

Here is Chet Baker singing "Everything Happens to Me"

Here are the police officers singing

I make a date for golf and you can bet your life it rains
I try to throw a party and the guy upstairs complains
I guess I'll go through life just catching colds and missing trains
Everything Happens to Me

The prisoners listen to the trumpet solo as they are kicked and spat on and spoken to in the cutest of voices

The prisoners play You're Dead for several hours

They do not know when the game will end

They do not know if they will ever be able to move

Everything happens to me

Lake Michigan, Scene 8

Why did you send me to the lake   father

Don't you know the white boys beat me here   father

They take my blood   father

They stab my leg   father

I am wearing the trousers you bought for me in the department store they made us burn down   father

They made us burn down the department store and told us to leave the state but they won't let me get my papers   father

My passport   the seals and signatures that document my national authenticity

They are khaki trousers   father

Once I wore them with my blue blazer   father   but now it doesn't matter because I am stuck here in this cage on the beach at the northern border of Chicago

There is a word   father   for when a boy kills his father

It's called patricide

And there is a word   father   for when a father kills his son

It's called filicide

But there is not a word for when a father oversees a gang of white boys stabbing into his son's leg

Shredding his son's pants

Flesh piercing blood puddling the white boys collecting my blood scraping my tongue cutting my hair stealing the parasites that live in the parasites that live in my body

Why do you let them take my blood   father

Why do you let them make me into a specimen   father

I know you know the answer to this question   father

It has to do with data   father

It has to do with the collection of large amounts of data   father

They want the blood of South American bodies   of Jewish bodies   olive bodies trashy bodies

They want my blood   father   but they don't want your blood

They don't want to punish you in the same way they punish me

They came to the house last week   father   and I protected you

I protected you when they came to interview me

Por qué piensas en mi sangre padre por qué vives en mi sangre padre

There was a knock on our door and they asked me my name and I said call me Daniel and they asked me to name names   father

They asked me for your name   father

They asked me where they could find you   father

Because they needed a side-by-side comparison of my skin against your skin   father

I said   I have a relationship with my father but it is voluntary

He did not force me to be his child

They did not care about the structure of our family

All they wanted to know was what my body looked like next to your body   father

How did I get such a dark body when you have such a light one

I chose to be dark   I told them

It was voluntary

I wanted to be darker   I wanted to look like a South American body

I told them this to save you   father

I never wanted to look like you   I told them

I did not want them to know what they already knew   father

Which is that you sleep with bodies from the South

They won't let me cross the border into Michigan Indiana or Iowa even though I have papers

We need proof of the boy's authenticity   say the authoritative bodies   we need proof that his blood is our blood and not their blood

You collected my blood for them   father

My little face is breaking into pieces   father

Por qué piensas en mi piel no hay nada aquí para comer   father

Why do you think of my skin when there's nothing to eat here   father

I eat foam and rocks

The grass the weeds the things I eat   father

I dance too fast   father

I dance too fast and the music plays too slow   father

The beach is rotting   father

The obscenity of the rotting beach   father

We will break the wind and melt into the variegated data   father

The aggregated data   the segregated data   the flagellated data

I am a slender series of attached cells   father

My data is thrashing in spume and fungi at the bottom of the lake   father

At the bottom of a rotten lake where my face my skin my bones my data will disappear

First my face will disappear

Then my neck my chest my hips my thighs my knees my feet my toes my blood my faceless face this lust   father

This emptiness   father

This hollow cave in my ribs   father

My death rattle   father

The eternal disappearance of my degenerate privatized flesh   father

Lake Michigan, Scene 9

The light is purple on the lake as the sun rises over the skyscrapers in downtown Chicago

We march to the beach while the soldiers point their guns at us

They tell us we must give thanks our mouths are not filled with dirt

They tell us we must give thanks our mouths are not filled with tornadoes

They tell us we must give thanks our mouths are not filled with foam

The beach is scattered with bodies and we must give thanks we are not among them

But we do not give thanks

So they beat us

And when we thank them for beating us they dunk our heads in the water and shove dead birds into our hands and we pray and they punch us and kick us and tell us we should be thankful our gums are not black and shrunken

You should be thankful your tongues are not swollen   that your arms have not fallen off   that you have not been tossed into a fire   off a building   or into the middle of a frozen sea

And they like how we pray

So they beat us

And we thank them and they say what else are you thankful for and we do not know what else we should be thankful for and they tell us we should be thankful for the food we eat

They take food from starving bodies and give it to us

We should be thankful for the water we drink

They take water from thirsty bodies and we drink it

We don't want to drink their water

But our bodies give us no choice

And we thank them for allowing us to eat when others starve

And we thank them for allowing us to drink when others dehydrate

And we thank them for allowing us to die slowly when others die quickly

Pray for your comrades   they say

Pray for your mothers and fathers and one by one they dunk our heads into the water and when we re-emerge we see the purple light over the skyscrapers

We feel the race wind and we smell the rancid stench of the decomposing bodies we have become

We feel their race war in our mouths   bubbling   foaming   festering

And we are silent

So they beat us

And there are cracks in the sky and we see god in the cracks and we see whiteness in the cracks and we see our bodies recomposing in the cracks and we see the war turning into another war and we see the mayor and we see angels and we see our bodies dissolving and we see the tornado in our mouths turning into a river and we see a hailstorm and eyelids blinking over our bodies and our bodies become our houses and our houses are exploding and as they explode we explode and we see the lake opening in the cracks in the sky and it is only the beginning of the war   a voice says

And we thank you   we sing

We thank you for not killing us through combustion

We thank you for not attaching a heated metal contraption to our head and exploding us

We thank you for not pouring molten metal into our throats or ears

We thank you for not waterboarding us

We thank you for not boiling us

We thank you for not stoning us

We thank you for not shoving tubes into our mouths and filling our bodies with vitamins and minerals

We thank you for letting us scoop each other out of our holes

We thank you for not running us over with your trucks or electrocuting us

We thank you for not abandoning us in a desert

We thank you for keeping our bodies from dehydrating and we thank you for keeping our bodies from shrinking

We remember when we were so small we could barely see the sun

We remember when we were so small we could barely see the lake and we ask the police officers to forgive us

And when they forgive us they beat us and when they beat us they pray for us and when they pray for us we pray for ourselves and we think of the humans we once loved

We think of our parents and our lovers and our children

And we see our friends in the cracks in the sky and our bodies are shaking and they beat us so we don't shake and there are floods now in our mouths and we are crushing each other

We are the hostages we prayed we would not become

And on the loudspeaker a man says

This is only war

This is only the beginning of the war

And he tells us the world is breathing in its own shit and collapsing

And he tells us that this war is a war of friendship   of camaraderie   civility   and love

And we remember how they took our bodies and forced us to confess to be other than who we are

And we remember the water they dunked our heads in and we remember when the Chicago Police told us we had lost the right to be public bodies and we would never have enough money to buy ourselves back from the bank

And we sing about the many ways there are to be dead

And we sing about the many ways there are to love and we refuse to collapse into nothing

We refuse to collapse into the privatized cellars of humanity and there is no name for where we will go when we refuse because there are only names for private bodies and we say let us collapse   for once and for all let us collapse   but our bodies refuse and we thank the police officers for this gift called life   and we are hundreds of years old in our bones   and we are helpless babies in our skin   and we sing and pray so that someday soon we might permanently collapse   because the beginning of the war is endless

It is always the beginning of war

The great virtue of a free market system is that it does not care what color people are; it only cares whether they can produce something you want to buy. It is the most effective system we have discovered to enable people who hate one another to deal with one another and help one another.

—Milton Friedman

y por las calles la sangre de los niños
corría simplemente, como sangre de niños.

—Pablo Neruda

The police shooting boys are like police shooting boys

And the nazis burning Jews are like nazis burning Jews

And the police protecting nazis are like police protecting nazis

And the prisoners who are tortured are like prisoners who are tortured

And the psychologists overseeing torture are like psychologists overseeing torture

And the mayor privatizing prisons is like the mayor privatizing prisons

And the rule of law being suspended is like the rule of law being suspended

And the broken prisoners on the beach are like broken prisoners on the beach

I dream I am pregnant and my baby is a revolutionary plan to destroy the global economy

And my baby is like a baby with a bullet in its mouth who is like a baby with a bullet in its mouth who is like a baby with a bullet in its mouth

And the disappearing public employees are like disappearing public employees

And the puddle of vomit from a tortured prisoner is like a puddle of vomit from a tortured prisoner

And the hunger of an actual child is the hunger of an actual child

And the basic function of the economy is the basic function of the economy

And the politically impossible is the politically inevitable

And the bourgeois savages are like bourgeois savages

And the bourgeois savages who do not see themselves as savages are like bourgeois savages who do not see themselves as savages

And the bodies that are expropriated for private purposes are like bodies expropriated for private purposes

And when they disappear into the pinhole of capital they disappear into the abyss of capital

And when they disappear into the abyss of capital there is that silence when everyone refuses to act because they are too concerned with their own material health to care about the broken body of another

And the wasted food on the beach is like wasted food on the beach

And the starving children who are not allowed to eat the wasted food on the beach are like starving children who are not allowed to eat wasted food on the beach

And the bourgeois savages do not notice the broken bodies until they are beaten in their bourgeois backyards

And they say how dare you use my backyard to beat this broken body   I will look away if only you don't beat them in my backyard

And they say one broken body in my backyard doesn't count for anything and they are like people who think that one broken body doesn't count for anything

And a massacre at a Black church is a massacre at a Black church

And a massacre at an elementary school is a massacre at an elementary school

And the nazis with torches are like nazis with torches

And the police who kill are like police who kill

And the dying sand is like dying sand

And the refugee arrested for speaking the wrong language is a prisoner who never learns to speak the right language

And the bomb is like a bomb and the anesthetic is like anesthetic

And the blankness of the city is like the blankness of the city

And the language of the riot is the language of the riot

And the blood of the silenced is like the blood of the silenced

And the blindness of the bourgeois savage is like a mouth that can't stop biting a body that refuses to die

Lake Michigan, Scene 11

15 men around a van from the Department of Streets and Sanitation

The men push from the side and back

The van is rocking up and down

It is starting to tip

More men come to the side

9 pushes and it bounces but it doesn't quite flip and a bunch of men walk away as a horn blares loudly as if telling the men to stop

The mechanics of flipping a van over

Push until it's bouncing and once it bounces high enough lift from the bottom

11 more pushes and the van falls over onto the driver's side and there is a celebratory whoop as the men walk away knowing that no one is ahead of his time

A riot is a thing that decides how it is to be done

And who among these men wants to consider the very long history of how he has ever acted or how he has ever felt

What do they see when they look at the flipped-over van

The flipped-over van   the long pole busting the glass   the fire and the smoke bombs
the men and women with scarves over their faces taking what they can from the
municipal vehicles

The war that has formed their relationship to the composition of the city

The war that has formed the police officers' punitive relationship to the bodies that
occupy the city

The innocence of rudimentary violence as the devouring power of negation

Who are the bodies when the bodies are not flipping over the van

What do they wish to compose when they are not composing the destruction of the city

What do they feel about the city and its refusal to absorb them

What do they feel about the state and its desire to spit them out

How will they be absorbed and how will they be ejected

There is distribution and there is despair and there are the things we decide to see when
we look and the things we decide to see when we shield our eyes from the pain

What else is there to be done once the van has been flipped over

What steps do we need to take to create lasting structural changes in our neighborhood
our city   our nation

How many vans should be flipped over and in what order

They ponder these questions with screams flames and poles jammed into the glass of
cars and storefronts   jammed into the burden to transact   compose   destroy

Lake Michigan, Scene 12

Our blood was like our blood and their boots in our eyes were like boots in our eyes and they kicked us even though we did nothing

Their bullets were like bullets and their hearts were like hearts and they clubbed us even though we did nothing

The dead boys kept dying and the beach kept swallowing us and they beat us even though we did nothing

The cops kicked us even though we did nothing

They threw us in the shit and kicked the shit out of us

They smashed bottles on us

They tear-gassed us

They beat us on the beach

They beat us at the mayor's house

They beat us at Banana Republic

They beat us at the Apple Store

They beat us in Chicago   on a sunny day in February

They beat us in Chicago   on a rainy day in November

The international observers watched as they beat us and saw nothing

They tasered us

We scaled a wall in a cloud of smoke and they beat us

We fell into the smoke and they fucked up our faces   our eyes   our teeth

Here are the broken bodies carried out on stretchers

Here are the broken boys with burned-up faces

Will their broken faces be burned and broken forever

Will the abandoned bodies be burned and broken forever

And what will we do with the broken bodies when they are no longer there to be broken

What will we do with the nightsticks when there are no more cops to swing them

Push aside the hollow bodies   say the authorities

Stick them into the cages with the other broken bodies   with the other broken meat

And there will be nowhere to go because there will be nowhere to go

Don't move   broken bodies

Don't go   broken bodies

Break slowly   broken bodies   the beginning of your bodies must die

Lake Michigan, Scene 13

The police came but we confused them with terrorists

The terrorists came and we confused them with our neighbors

And there were nationalists who spoke to the early Americans about love

And the early Americans spoke to the economists about protecting the homeland

And the economists spoke to the nazis about fiduciary responsibility

And the nazis spoke to the journalists about hope

And the journalists wrote about the disaster and we said no no our bodies don't look the way you say they look   they are not filled with yellow clots   they are filled with purple holes   our skin is not ashen   it's fluorescent   our bones are not broken they are mending

And they took away our pills and said   be happier

And they took away our doctors and said   be healthier

And our perspective shifted from we to I   from they to you

And they shaved our heads and burned us and asked us to find the perfect word to describe the water

And the lake looked like a filthy mop and we searched for the perfect word and I said disaster

And they searched for the perfect word and they said peace

And they said listen listen   if you stand over here the voice of god says one thing in the wind and over there the voice of god says something completely different

And the authoritative body said the city has a collective challenge ahead   not with our words but with our deeds   in our everyday work   whether it's instructing or leading or guiding

We must continue to move the needle   we must significantly push the envelope   we must think outside the box the bubble the vacuum

We have only scratched the surface of our full potential and we are ready to cement this chapter in the city of Chicago's history

We must be the highest performing city in America

Do I believe that's doable said the authoritative body to the functionaries   absolutely absolutely   it can get done   we are not there yet but it can get done and it will get done so let us build a lasting culture of accountability to sustain our excellence

I look forward to the beach becoming a new beach said the mayor   to the lake becoming a new lake

God is a tough act to follow   the mayor said to the functionaries

The mayor is a tough act to follow   the nazis said to the nationalists

The nazis are a tough act to follow   the nationalists said to the economists

The burning lake is a tough act to follow

We must provide our citizens with a transformative experience said the mayor to our bodies as they broke on the shore

We do not want to merely retain your bodies   we want to recondition your bodies

We want you to know that our collective commitment to your development reflects the city's collective commitment to what is small   to what cannot be seen   to what cannot be heard and nothing is more important than you

Nothing is more important than your bodies

You have the most face time with your children

You have the most face time with those to whom we deliver our services and you are not alone in this crucial work

Your bodies are our machines and every day we will use your teeth your eyes your hair

But right now there's too much sand in your mouth

There's a lightning storm in your mouth

There's too much light in your eyes

There are swarms of bees in your nose

This is not what the city intended for your body

This is not what the city intended for your collective experience

The rain that falls is trash and the bus can only get you home if the door opens

I speak to you today   said the authoritative body   about social security

But what I really mean is that the windows only appear to be covered in shit

Look closely and you will see the horizon   it only appears to be covered in blood

Look closely at the lake   it only appears to be colonized with E. coli

Look closely at the healing body   it only appears to be covered in wounds

I do not know your name or your number

I only know that your body is the burden   the border   between light and the balance
of time

Lake Michigan, Scene 14

The dead man asks me where I want to fly

And I say I don't want to fly anywhere

I want to stay here and defend my people

And the dead man says who are your people

And I point to the list of the names of the missing people and I am clubbed over the head with a wooden oar and dragged away by the police to the overstuffed prison camp on the beach and I think that survival must be vulgar and I am taken to a coroner's office and there are tools on the cold metal table they lay me on and there are men in lab coats and there are attorneys and there is paperwork and they lay the paperwork over my body and someone comes to sign something and they sign the paper then a bureaucrat signs my leg and a nurse signs my leg and an attorney signs my leg and I come to understand that my leg is a legal document that will be filed in accordance with the necessary procedures needed to classify the remains of the dead

Outside the coroner's office the guard paces back and forth   inside I am the specimen

We are in a secret facility on the beaches of Lake Michigan   on the northern end of Chicago

This is where they take the bodies when they have finally stopped moving them from one holding cell to another

They move us from one police station to another until we are taken here as I have been taken here and tied to a radiator and my body burns and there are officers with guns pointing at my head asking me to confess to crimes I know nothing about and they turn the heat up on the radiator and I cannot take the burn any longer so I tell them I am guilty

I tell them I have done the things they say I have done

I have committed crimes against humanity   murdered   kidnapped   transported small children from one part of the city to another

I am on the coroner's table and a priest comes to offer me absolution and I tell him I don't want it because I am Jewish and they tell me I have no choice and the priest blesses my body so that I can leave the never-ending trauma of earth for the paradisiacal joy of heaven

Then they choke me until I die

And I am lying on the table dead and once more learning how to suffer

And I am lying with the other corpses and we are sick of being examined

We are sick of being identified

We are sick of being prodded and poked and groped and a man with a camera and notebook says by way of explanation that this is only war

And for a second we are nothing at all and then we remember that once we were a strategic operation   that once we were emblems of the state and we remember we have always been immigrants and we remember how they stoned us when we spoke our language and we remember the mobs of adolescents who stood over us   who spat on us and pissed in our faces and told us to never speak our words again

And the voice of the man who takes photos of our bodies says   remember   this is only war

And another voice says   remember   this is only Chicago

And we are the corpses they stack on the beach

And we are the bodies that will be mauled by dogs

And we are the memory

And we are thousands of years old and they destroy us

They execute us even though we are already dead

And they store us in a memorial that will open dozens of years from now   a memorial where they will display our broken bodies to remind the future citizens of Chicago that this is only war and that forever we have always been dead

Lake Michigan, Scene 15

They bring in the Chicago bodies   the Nordic bodies   the Chilean bodies   to play music for us   to accompany the wind and the waves

They circle us

They dance for us

They think I might have some power to release some bit of life from the lake

But I have no power

I am nearly as powerless as they are

It's just that the things I am commanded to do are easier than the things the pale bodies are commanded to do

I am commanded to guard the Puerto Rican bodies   the Cuban bodies   the Peruvian bodies   the French and Italian and German bodies   the Armenian and Slovenian and Algerian bodies   the moldy dusty white and beige UnitedStatesian bodies   as they move from barracks to bathroom   from bathroom to cafeteria   from cafeteria to solitary confinement unit   etc.

An imprisoned boy with a ukulele approaches us   smiling the way they force us to smile so that the international observers can see how happy the incarcerated bodies are here in Chicago

What do you mean   happy

I mean bread

Every morning the privatized Chicagoans   the white   the brown   the immigrant
wake up and there is an enormous loaf of bread in the barracks

And a sharp knife for them to slice the bread and split it equally

Every morning everyone gets a slice of bread

And in the evening   a tomato

And in the afternoon   crackers

And sometimes they take the loneliest red bodies to a clearing in the forest

Their rancid bodies smell like turpentine

And it is good   we are told   to convalesce among the pine needles and there are still
ducks there   there are still some deer and even further away there are sheep and cows
and horses even though the authoritative bodies have done everything they can to
remove their stables   their pastures   their menacing animal influence

Thank you for the description

But some things are still unclear

Who do the white bodies belong to   who do the beige bodies belong to   who owns
the red and yellow bodies   where do the immigrants sleep at night   to whom do they
cry and pray

A: they are poor and opaque and when they crossed over from one civilization into
another no one knew what color they were

Q: Since you have a certain level of privilege vis-à-vis the broken bodies   the
privatized bodies   the socially toxic Caucasian bodies   since they talk to you from
their re-education cells in the barracks   perhaps one of them has told you exactly who

it was that betrayed you   who turned you in to the authorities   who sold your body to the administrators of the rotten carcass economy

A: My mother betrayed me

My father betrayed me

My sister wrote a note and signed it and said I was a parasitic   infected   South American body

My family did not want me to find them

They were escaping and could not fit me in the truck with the breathing bodies they needed to smuggle out and trade for vitamins and minerals

So they left me here and I thought they were dead

But they did not die

They merely abandoned me

I know this because when I was arrested for trying to flee the whitened campgrounds the authoritative bodies locked me in a cell and forced me to watch the video of my family giving their exit interview

Where will you go

        The County of X

Who will take care of your boy

        Doesn't matter

Why do you not want him to go with you

        No response

What animals will you take

All the animals

What personal effects will you carry

Just the essentials

What will you hope for

Peace

What do you seek to achieve

We want the lake to reappear
We want the beach to bloom again
We want the grass in the field to be green

And my family does not cry as they take their exit

And the wardens hit me on the mouth when I finish watching this

And my lips swell and there is blood and I fall to the floor and they scream at me until I get up and they kick me again

And the authoritative body says   we own the water now

Fuck your family

We own the sand now   the river   the rocks

And they begin to bury me

And as they bury me I hear the voice of the mayor

I hear the wardens filling up the privatized bathtub of dawn with as many broken Central American bodies as they can find

I hear the voice of my cowardly blue father

I hear the immigrants being whipped above ground   I hear laughter and music from the viewing areas outside the cages in the containment center

And I hear   son   we will give you the lake if you promise to stay underground forever

We will give you the beach   son   if you promise to dig yourself into the trenches and to never join a world that's not yellow or beige or purple

Take the white snow now   son

Take the black silence now   son

Son   the white snow and the black silence are yours

Take this purple night now   son

Take this shadow and breathe before they bury you deeper than you'll ever want to go

It's roomy down there   and restful   and you will never cry for the light

Lake Michigan, Scene 16

Hate in the river

Hate in the lake

Hate in the hunger

Hate in the mouth forced to talk

Hate in the body forced to crawl

The Chicago liberal gives birth to the fascist

Pays the fascist for its service to the city then screeches when the fascist punches him in the throat

Loads the gun for the cop who shoots into a car full of teenagers

Starves the city

Boards up its schools

Disappears its nurses

Liquefies into the sand to hide from the race war he created

Pays the immigrants to clean the river

Hates the fuck out of the union

At dusk   the lake kicks the shit out of our bodies

At dusk   the torture-boy takes his orders from the liberal who employs him

At dusk   they line us up and tell us about the beauty of the trees   the beauty of the
leaves   the beauty of the sand   the beauty of the water   the beauty of the skyline
the beauty of the wind   the beauty of our hate and fear

At dusk   the savage bark from the tooth of the toothless   the mouth of the mouthless
the bones of the collapsed   the ashen moldy ground

I bought my house

They took my house

They moved out when I moved in

They closed shop when I moved in

My house went underwater

The lake wouldn't stop rising

The beach wouldn't stop collapsing

And my house went underwater

And my house sat empty as the bank told me to find a new house

I bought it I bought it you don't own it it's under the water your house is under the water

The body of the bodiless   the mouth of the mouthless   the tongue of the tongueless

The broken bodies crawl to the border

The Chicago liberals escort them to the suburbs

They don't need to catalog the plight of the bodies they break when the end of the world is always beginning

They call us dystopianists and we vomit

They call us realists and we vomit

They call us surrealists and we vomit

They want to locate our reality outside of their reality but their houses are not under the water

Their bodies are not under the beach

Their houses are not filled with blank

Their memories are not filled with blank

Their children do not have blue skin

They are much less hideous than we are

Their institutions have never been as ugly as ours

We know where we stand with the cops and the nazis

What's better

To know or not know when your ass is going to be beaten

I was born with an ugly mouth and a bag of bullets in it

I was born with an ugly head and a ball of slime on it

The cannibals are less ugly than we are

The birds on the beach are broken and drenched in disease

Lake Michigan, Scene 17

It's not enough to feel shame

It's not enough to starve

It's not enough to be dead when others are more dead

I drink coffee in the morning among murderers

My neighbors love nooses and bullets

The grass refuses to die

The city keeps reappearing

Why won't it disappear forever

The streets were better when they were dried-up rivers

The rivers were better when they were gurgling swamps

We live in the blankest of times   and I can sense love in the mouths of my captors

I can sense love in the eyes of my captors

I can sense love in the way they touch me

But it's an illusion

They would kill us all as quickly as they could if it weren't for the United Nations

The lake keeps disappearing and there is too much light

We can't see the lake because all we see is light

And the light is the water they dump us in

And they dump us in the water and they count us

They count us but they can't get the numbers right so they count us again and again

And we whisper to our broken bodies:

Don't let them tell you there's no use in speaking

Don't let them tell you there's no use in being silent

Don't let them tell you there's no use in fighting back when they beat us

Don't let them tell you there's no use in not fighting back when they beat us

Don't let them tell you there's no use in laughing even when nothing is funny

I died in Chicago on a beach where the broken bodies are sealed in plastic   where the broken bones are covered with cement

And the cockroaches are swimming in puddles of our spit and blood

They are swimming in the things that are forced out of our bodies

But I have light in my eyes and today I have hope

I can hypnotize anyone who touches me the wrong way

Which is everyone   because no one who is kind is allowed to touch me

I live in crate #17

I will soon be shipped across the border   to the financiers who own me

But how much of me do they own

And who owns the blood that drips from my wounds into the hemorrhaging sky that can't withstand its own illness

The wound-sky and the race wind it dumps on us

We live in the blankest of times

Lake Michigan, Scene 18

The beaches are filled with cages

And the cages are filled with bodies

And the bodies are filled with burdens

And the burdens consume the bodies

And the bodies do not know to whom they owe their life

I drop my body on the sand and someone tells me to pick it up

I drop to the sand to pick up my body and someone tells me to steal more hair   to steal more flesh   to steal more bones   to steal more fingers

I tell them I cannot risk contaminating the data

I tell them that if I steal more hair then the data will not be clean

I tell them I cannot touch my own body out of fear of contaminating the data

I have a virus   I say

I am contagious   I say

No salt in my body   I say   no heat in my blood

The sand is dying slowly

It turns into a wall and in the wall there is a nook and in the nook there is light and in light there is god and in god there is nothing and in nothing there is hope and in hope there is abandonment and in abandonment there is wound and in wound there is nation and in nation there are bones and in bones there is time and in time there is light and in light there are numbers and in numbers there are codes and in codes there are mountains and in mountains there are bodies searching for bones and in the mountains there are tunnels and in the tunnels there is so much festering garbage

The men in uniform take the garbage away but they have a hard time distinguishing the garbage from the people so they scoop it all up and carry us into the next morning

And in the next morning there is a confession

I have put my burdens in the wrong body

I have framed my burdens in the wrong language

I have staked my burdens to the wrong nation

I need medicine to sleep

I need medicine to stop the shrieking in my ears

I need medicine to make the Chicago corpses turn into hydrangeas

I need medicine to make the immigrants turn into butterflies

I need an injection to make the bureaucrats turn into terrorists

It is raining again on Lake Michigan

Some say it is raining bodies   but really it is raining trash

The trash they bomb us with explodes when it lands near our bodies

And our bodies are tornadoes

And the joke turns into a mystery novel about how god keeps his hands from shaking when he is about to destroy the universe

I need my burdens   sing the bodies on the beach

I fight for my burdens   scream the bodies on the beach

I know the blankness of my burdens is a battle for love and country

I know the blankness of my burdens is a coda to the death of the city

I don't know why I can't see the moon anymore

I can't see the stars or the sky anymore

I don't even bother to look up

(1) Aimé Césaire's epigraph is from *Notebook of a Return to My Native Land*, translated by Mireille Rosello with Annie Pritchard.

(2) On February 24, 2015, Spencer Ackerman of the *Guardian* published an investigative article titled "The Disappeared: Chicago Police Detain Americans at Abuse laden 'Black-Site.'" The article told the story of Homan Square, a secret interrogation facility on the West Side of Chicago. Ackerman's article asserts that Homan Square is a secret police torture chamber. According to the article, Homan Square's abuses include:

- Keeping arrestees out of official booking databases
- Beating by police, resulting in head wounds
- Shackling for prolonged periods
- Denying attorneys access to the "secure" facility
- Holding people without legal counsel for between 12 and 24 hours, including people as young as 15

Flint Taylor, "the civil-rights lawyer most associated with pursuing the notoriously abusive Area 2 police commander Jon Burge," links the origins of these practices in Chicago back to the 1970s: "Back when I first started working on torture cases and started representing criminal defendants in the early 1970s, my clients often told me they'd been taken from one police station to another before ending up at Area 2 where they were tortured. . . . And in that way the police prevent their family and lawyers from seeing them until they could coerce, through torture or other means, confessions from them."

As the *Guardian's* Spencer Ackerman, Zach Stafford, and Joanna Walters report:

> from 1972 through 1991, Burge and officers under his command tortured more than 100 African Americans largely in impoverished sections of Chicago's South Side in a systematic regime of violence and intimidation. Men in custody were subjected to electric shocks burns and mock executions, among other brutal acts, predominantly in order to extract confessions. . . . Burge ran a group of rogue detectives known as the Midnight Crew who led the violence. There are allegations that officers used suffocation on those in their custody and forced men to play "Russian roulette." . . . Burge was fired in 1993 but was never charged with crimes directly stemming from the violence. Before the statute of limitations ran out, he was convicted in 2010 of obstruction of justice and perjury in relation to a civil lawsuit alleging that he tortured citizens. He subsequently served four and a half years in prison before being released in 2014, and continues to draw a police pension.

(3) "Gutting social welfare and privatizing public assets have become the new urban dogma. [Privatizing] bridges, parking meters, public parking garages, schools, hospitals, and public housing, while driving down the cost of labor through deregulation, outsourcing unionized jobs, [and] casualized and contingent labor. To deal with the contradictions produced by neoliberal policies in Chicago and nationally, the privatizing state is also a punitive state that polices and contains immigrants, homeless people, the dispossessed, and low-income communities of color, particularly youth, and their political resistance. Chicago is notorious for its police torture scandals and brutal policing of African American and Latino communities. In short, neoliberal urbanism has set in motion new forms of state-assisted economic, social and spatial inequality, marginality, exclusion and punishment." Pauline Lipman, "Contesting the City: Neoliberal Urbanism and the Cultural Politics of Education Reform in Chicago." *Discourse: Studies in the Cultural Politics of Education* 32 (2011).

(4) Simone de Beauvoir's epigraph to Act 1 is from Lois Wille's *Forever Open, Clear, and Free: The Struggle for Chicago's Lakefront*.

(5) Milton Friedman's epigraph to Act 2 is from a 1991 lecture titled "Why Government Is the Problem."

(6) Pablo Neruda's epigraph to Act 2 is from the poem "Explico algunas cosas" from *España en el corazón* (1937).

(7) "The discovery of personal whiteness among the world's peoples is a very modern thing,—a nineteenth and twentieth century matter, indeed. The ancient world would have laughed at such a distinction. The Middle-Ages regarded skin color with mild

curiosity; and even up into the eighteenth century we were hammering our national manikins into one, great, Universal Man, with fine frenzy which ignored color and race even more than birth. Today we have changed all that, and the world in a sudden, emotional conversion has discovered that it is white and by that token, wonderful!" W. E. B. Du Bois, *Darkwater: Voices from within the Veil.*

(8) This book would not exist without the writing of James Baldwin, Bertolt Brecht, Gwendolyn Brooks, Aimé Césaire, Don Mee Choi, Kim Hyesoon, Pablo Neruda, Cesar Vallejo, and Raúl Zurita, among many others.

(9) Many thanks to Broc Rossell, many thanks to Rachel Galvin for reading multiple drafts of this book, for making it better!

(10) We live in the blankest of times!

ACKNOWLEDGMENTS

Many thanks to the editors of the following publications for including earlier versions of some of these scenes from *Lake Michigan*:

Bathhouse, Boundary 2, Boston Review, Cream City Review, Fence, Inkwell, Lana Turner, Matter Monthly, Seedings, TriQuarterly, and *Virgina Quarterly Review.*